This book is dedicated to all the medical heroes during Covid-19

Copyright © 2020 by Tiny Angel Press LTD.

All rights reserved.

No part of this book may be reproduced, stored in a retrieval system,
or transmitted in any form or by any means, electronic, mechanical, photocopying,
recording, scanning, or otherwise, without the prior written permission of the publisher.

https://themonster-series.com

Illustrations by Dmitry Chizhov

Thanks to author Karen McMillan for her assistance with this project.

ISBN: 978-1-8380713-0-1

In collaboration with Duckling Publishing and Chrissy Metge Ltd.
www.ducklingpublishing.com
www.chrissymetge.com

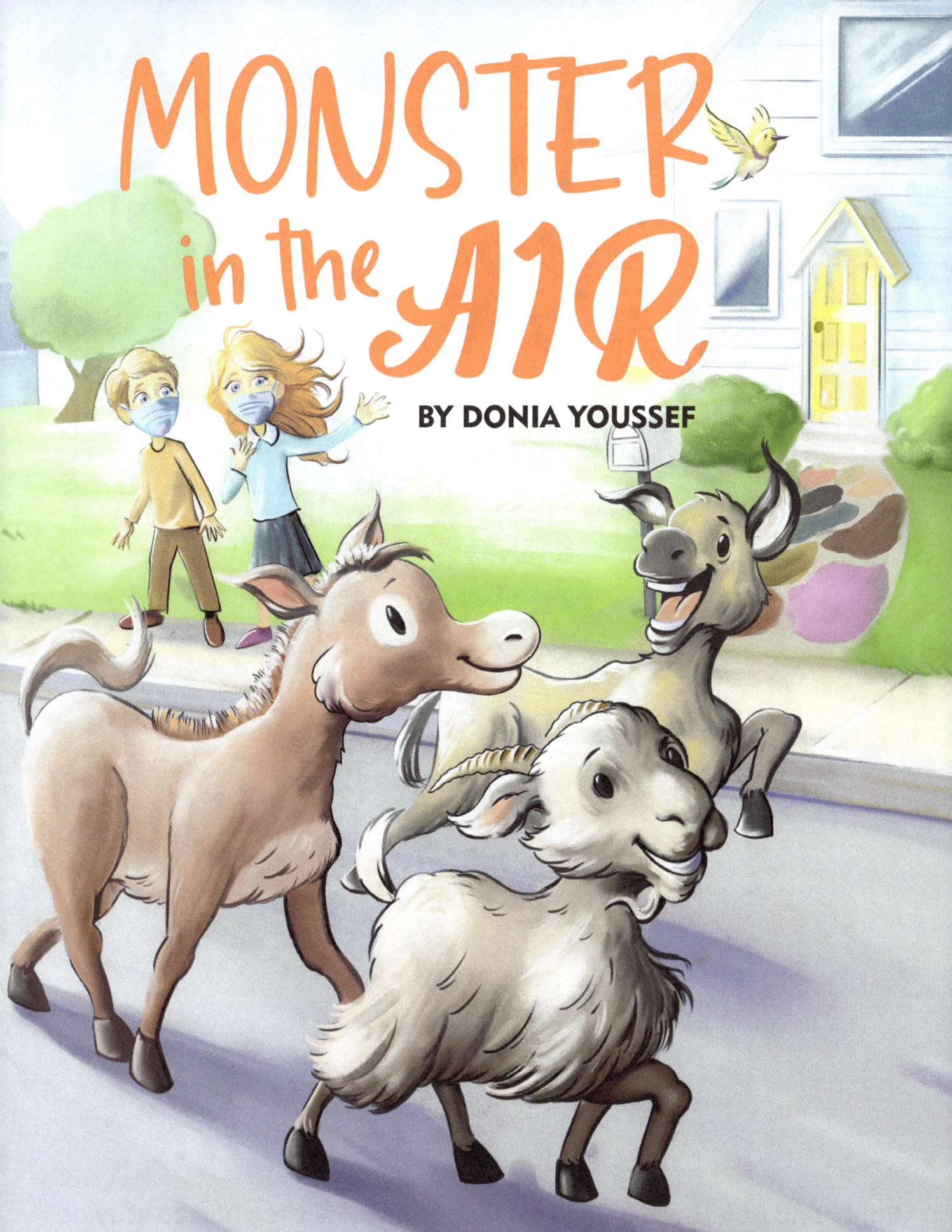

Emily and Ben loved going to school, but now they had to stay at home for a while.

Everyone in the family did, too. Mum and Dad were staying home from work, and everyone was doing their part.

It was fun to watch movies and play games together.

Mum and Dad said, "We know it's a bit of an adjustment to stay home, but we're going to make the best of it!"

First of all, Emily and Ben knew they had to keep clean. So washing with warm water and lots of soap was something they did each time they came in from outside.

And there were a lot of things to do!

Ben and Emily helped each other with their homework. And they even got to speak to their teacher and classmates online, seeing each other through video chat.

"That's so cool!" said Ben.

Mum and Dad came up with lots of fun things to do while they were at home with Ben and Emily.

"All right, kids," said Dad. "Who wants to build a treehouse?"

Emily and Ben's eyes brightened. "Me!" they both shouted.

Dad showed them how to choose wood and nails. And both Emily and Ben got a chance to swing a hammer. Soon, their new treehouse was looking like an actual house with doors and windows.

"And," said Mum, "we're going to make a little house for the birds, too."

Emily and Ben helped with that, and they both helped decorate their treehouse and birdhouse.

Soon, they were playing inside of their treehouse and feeding the birds.

Mum said, "Look, it's springtime, and the birds want to say hello!"

Since everyone was home more often, there were more things to try and experience.

"Can we plant a garden, mum?" asked Ben.

Mum, Ben, and Emily picked out things they wanted to plant in the garden. Ben chose herbs, Emily chose tomatoes and cucumbers, and Mum picked some pretty tulips.

Soon, they had prepared a place in the backyard. The dirt was dug, soil and fertiliser were put in, and all the seeds and little bulbs were planted.

Emily clapped and said, "I can't wait to watch them grow each day!"

"And," said Dad, joining them, "we will do our part in growing some of our own tasty fresh food."

Ben came running over, holding something high above his head.

"Look what I found in our garden!"

Emily ran over and said, "Ben! That's a wiggly worm!"

Ben and Emily giggled and ran back to look for more.

One day, after homework, Ben and Emily were playing a board game by the family room window with Mum and Dad.

"Ben, look at that!" said Emily, pushing her nose against the window.

Ben turned to see what all the commotion was, and there, outside on the street, was a little goat.

"Those are Farmer John's goats," said Dad. "They've gotten loose!"

Emily said, "Look, they're all running through the streets now! Poor Farmer John. They're looking at us now like we're the animals inside a cage!"

All the big hairy goats ran through the street, and then came running through Emily and Ben's garden.

"Uh, oh!" said Ben. "Watch out!"

Mum gasped. "Oh my, there go my tulips. A tasty snack for a lucky goat."

Emily and Ben giggled, but Mum shook her head.

"Don't worry, Mum!" they said. "We'll help you plant more."

Later that day, Emily and Ben went for a drive with Mum and Dad. They couldn't go inside to see Grandma and Grandad, but they could wave from the sidewalk.

"Here, you can talk on the phone," said Mum.

Emily and Ben spoke to Grandma and Grandpa through Mum's cell.

"And you wouldn't believe how many goats ran through the street!" they said brightly. "Oh, and poor Mum's tulips, they didn't stand a chance."

Grandma and Grandpa smiled and waved through their window.

"Well, now the animals are getting a nice taste of freedom with us inside all the time!" said Grandad. "Wait until you see Farmer John's donkeys, I bet they're ready to run, too!"

The next day, Emily and Ben wore their masks outside to help Mum plant new tulip bulbs.

"Look, there are Farmer John's donkeys like grandad said!"

Emily and Ben ran to see the donkeys running in the streets, staring at the humans in their funny-looking masks.

Later that day, Ben and Emily had a video chat with friends, and they told them all about the goats and donkeys.

So, it wasn't so bad staying at home and doing their part, keeping safe and everyone around them healthy.

"We can pull through this together!" said Ben.

And Emily smiled and held up a wiggly worm. "Yes, all of us! No matter how small... or slimy!"

THE END

Together we did it!

Additional information for children, parents, guardians and carers can be found below:
- CBBC Newsround – https://www.bbc.co.uk/newsround/52357230
- Childline – https://www.childline.org.uk/
- Young Minds – https://youngminds.org.uk/
- British psychological society – https://www.bps.org.uk/public
- The Samaritans – https://www.samaritans.org/
- Unicef – https://www.unicef.org.uk/

Supporting the NHS –

https://www.nhs.uk/using-the-nhs/about-the-nhs/get-involved-in-the-nhs/

Monster in the Air is one of several books I have written about the reality of facing serious illnesses.

After I released my first book, *The Monster in Mummy*, I became more and more involved with different charities and organisations. I realised there is so much as a society we could be doing to raise awareness and to help others facing certain challenges when it comes to our health.

I am so proud and humbled to be able to bring you these stories and help raise awareness that behind every serious illness is a real person

Donia Youssef, Author & Producer of *The Monster series*.

www.ingramcontent.com/pod-product-compliance
Lightning Source LLC
Chambersburg PA
CBHW080612300426
43661CB00143B/896